The Vikings in Scotland

Richard Dargie

WAYLAND

BBC EDUCATION SCOTLAND

The Vikings

Editor: Carron Brown
Designer: Joyce Chester

British Library Cataloguing in Publication Data
Dargie, Richard
The Vikings in Scotland
1. Vikings – Scotland – Juvenile Literature 2. Vikings
– Scotland – Social life and customs – Juvenile
literature 3. Scotland – History – To 1057 – Juvenile
Literature I. Title
941.1' 01' 089395

ISBN 0 7502 1570 4

Typeset by Joyce Chester
Printed and bound by B.P.C. Paulton Books,
Great Britain

The author would like to thank the Directorate of
Education, Culture and Sport of the Council of Europe,
Strasbourg and the In-Service Department of the
University of Upsalla for their support and their interest
in Viking studies.

Illustrations by Chris Ryley Illustration
Map artwork by Peter Bull Art on pages 7 and 8, and
Sallie Alane Reason on page 30

Picture Acknowledgements
The publishers gratefully acknowledge the permission of
the following to use their pictures in this book: Michael
Holford 14, 22; The Scottish Highland Picture Library
cover, *contents page*, 8, 26 (bottom), /Sue Anderson 5,
/HIE 19, /N. C. Mackenzie 27, /Eric Thorburn 10,
/Hugh Webster *title page*, 25, 26 (top); Ronald Sheridan,
Ancient Art and Architecture Collection 7, 9, 13, 14,
16, 18 (bottom), 23; Still Moving Picture Company 25,
/Angus Johnston 24; University of Oslo *cover*; Werner
Forman Archive 6, 15, 16, 17, 18 (top), 20, 23.

Norse, Northmen and Viking

The words **Norse** and **Northmen** are used to
describe the peoples of western and central
Scandinavia, who raided and settled in
northern Britain between AD 800 and 1150.

The word **Viking** is used to describe the
terrible, fearsome and cruel Norse warriors.
It comes from the Norse word 'a-viking'
which meant going on a raid. It was never used
by the Norse peoples to describe themselves.

in Scotland

Contents

The Attack on Iona AD 795

It was dawn. The abbey bell rang out across the island, calling the monks to worship. After prayer, the monks walked out silently from the chapel to the tasks of the day that lay ahead. None of them saw the sleek, wooden ship sailing into the bay from the north, or the warriors dragging their ship up on to the beach. Within minutes, the monks of Iona lay dead or were in chains. The great abbey of Iona was in flames.

Iona was one of the holiest places in the British Isles. The great Saint Columba had built his church there. The remains of his bones were kept on Iona in a holy box, called the Brecbannoch. An even greater treasure was held in the abbey library. For over 200 years, the Celtic monks of Iona had copied and stored histories, Bibles and other ancient writings.

Sea captains, passing from the kingdom of Dalriada to the kingdom of Man or to Ireland, often stopped at the island and asked for a blessing on their voyage. After their safe return, they gave grain, wine and other valuable goods to the monks of Iona.

To the raiders from the sea, Iona was a place of great riches and an easy target. They knew it was defended only by a few weak priests. The raiders had heard that the holy bones of an old Christian wizard called Columba were there. Christians said his bones had great powers.

The raiders first raided Iona in the year AD 795. They carried off some of the monks to their northern homelands to work as slaves in their fields. They took the jewelled covers from the abbey's books to sell or keep as trophies, but they failed to find the holy bones of Saint Columba. They returned three times, looking for the magic relics. In AD 825 they blood-eagled the leader of the monks, called Blathmac, cutting open his chest and ripping out his lungs. Yet the raiders were never to find the Brecbannoch. Instead, they discovered a rich and beautiful land, which they could conquer, settle and farm.

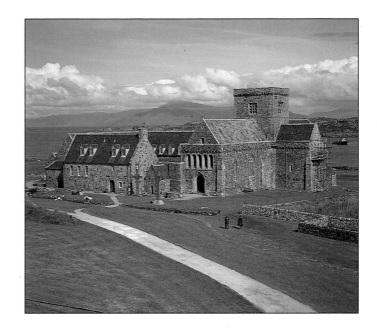

The holy abbey of Iona lies on a small island off the Scottish coast. It was a centre of learning between AD 600 and 800.

The Northmen and their Homeland

The raiders were the feared Northmen. Their longships were a dreaded sight along the coasts of Europe. The Northmen came from Norway, Sweden and Denmark – the lands of Scandinavia. They were skilful Germanic peoples. At home in Scandinavia they lived by farming and fishing. After AD 790, the Northmen began to travel across Europe by sea, to sell and buy goods, and to raid.

The Northmen of eastern Scandinavia were the Svea. They sailed across the Baltic Sea to the northern coasts of Poland and Germany. They travelled down the rivers of Russia towards the city of Micklagard. They settled in the growing towns of eastern Europe. As traders, warriors and princes, the Svea helped to build the first Russian city of Kiev.

The Danish Northmen, or Danes, traded and raided across northern Europe, mixing with the different peoples there. To win the Danes' friendship, the French king gave them a large area of farming land. This land is known as Normandy, the land of the Northmen. Thousands of Danes attacked and conquered the weak kingdoms of England, and settled there in the years after AD 866.

The Norse or Norwegians were perhaps the most adventurous of the Northmen. These Northmen raided Iona in AD 795. They raided and settled in Scotland, Ireland, and the islands of Orkney and Shetland. They also sailed far north and west, discovering Iceland, Greenland and America.

This wooden carving of a Northman was made about AD 850. It was found in a Viking grave in Norway.

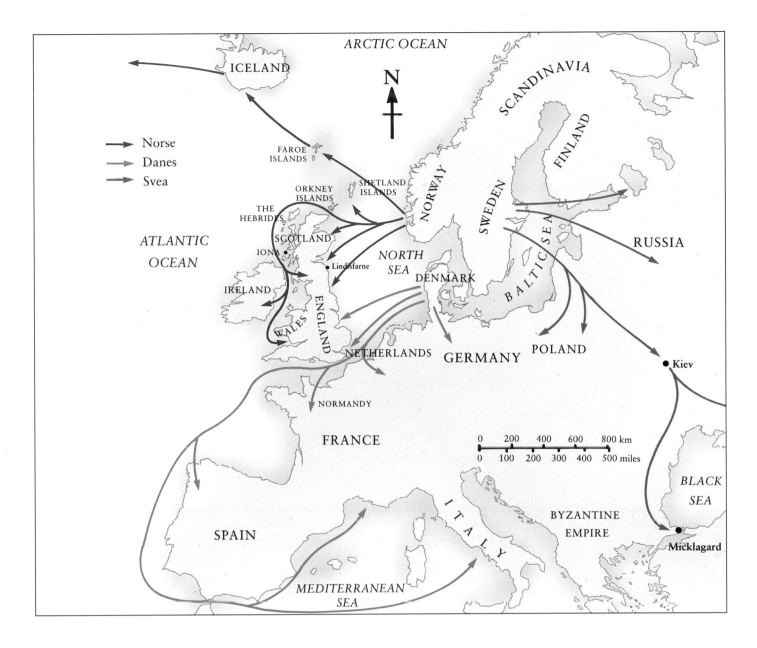

Map of Viking routes.

We do not know why the Northmen left Scandinavia. Perhaps the raiders were running away from new, strong kings that had come to power in their homelands. Or perhaps the peoples of Scandinavia were short of food. There was little farming land and the summer growing season was short.

We do know that the Northmen were soon feared across Europe. Their ships were light, fast and strong. As warriors, the Northmen were tough and brave. As traders, they were clever and successful. They were also pagans who worshipped old mysterious gods. Christians all over Europe gathered to say the same prayer: '*From the fury of the Northmen, deliver us, O Lord …*'

Scotland in the Dark Ages

Historians sometimes call the years between AD 400 and 800 the Dark Ages. This is because we do not know much about the people who lived in Britain then. At this time, Scotland was a land of marshes, moorland and mountains. Much of the country was covered by the thick Caledonian pine forest where hardly anyone lived. There were no towns.

Most people lived in small farm villages that were clustered in the glens below a hill-fort.

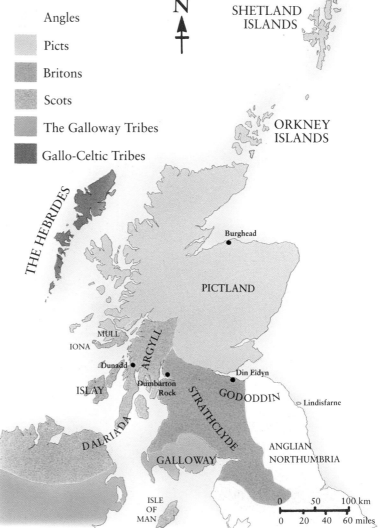

Angles
Picts
Britons
Scots
The Galloway Tribes
Gallo-Celtic Tribes

N

SHETLAND ISLANDS

ORKNEY ISLANDS

THE HEBRIDES

Burghead

PICTLAND

MULL
IONA
ISLAY
DALRIADA
ARGYLL
Dunadd
Dumbarton Rock
STRATHCLYDE
GALLOWAY
Din Eidyn
GODODDIN
Lindisfarne
ANGLIAN NORTHUMBRIA

ISLE OF MAN

0   50   100 km
0 20 40 60 miles

Left: This is a carving on a Pictish standing stone in the Orkney Islands. It shows three Pictish warriors marching into battle.

Above: Scotland in the Dark Ages.

There were several different peoples living in Dark Age Scotland. The people who lived in the north of Scotland were called Picts. The Picts were skilled metalworkers and farmers. Their name comes from an ancient word *pett* which means a piece of land. One of their strongholds was the fortress on the coast at Burghead in Morayshire. Many mysterious Pictish-stone carvings and inscriptions can still be seen today.

The early peoples of Scotland liked to decorate stone crosses with detailed carvings.

Several peoples lived in the south of Scotland. The oldest British tribes had fortresses at Din Eidyn, which we now know as Edinburgh, and at Dumbarton. The Lothian district of modern Scotland takes its name from one of the Britons' leaders, King Lot.

We know of kingdoms called Gododdin and Strathclyde. In the south, Galloway was a wild borderland where many old tribes and new invaders lived and mixed together.

After AD 450, these ancient tribes were slowly pushed out of their homelands by two groups of powerful newcomers. One of these were the Angles of Northumbria. They conquered most of northern England and spread into south-eastern Scotland. In time, the Angles became Christian and were known as English. They were a cultured people who brought many new ideas and skills with them.

At the same time, an important tribe moved into south-western Scotland. They crossed the sea from their homeland in Ireland to Argyll and the western islands of Islay and Mull. Their capital was the rock fortress of Dunadd in mid-Argyll. They were a Christian people and spoke Gaelic. They called their new kingdom Dalriada, but were known by their neighbours as *scotii*. This old Latin word means robbers. Their kingdom became known as Scotia or Scotland.

Norse Life in Scotland

The first Northmen came to Scotland as raiders. After AD 800, many Scandinavian people came as merchants, farmers and settlers. They settled in the far north and west of the Scottish mainland, and in the many islands along these coasts.

In many ways, the land was like Scandinavia – rough and mountainous, with long sea lochs which cut deep into the coast. Only a few Celtic people, the Gaels or the Picts, lived in these lands, so there was space for the Northmen to settle. Above all, the Northmen could travel quickly from the Shetland Islands to Argyll by sea.

By AD 850, many Northmen had settled in Scotland with their families. They wore clothes made from simple materials. Their clothes had to keep them warm and last a long time. Men wore woollen cloaks, tunics and breeches. Next to their skin they wore long vests of linen. They hung swords and purses from their belts. Women wore linen shifts under woollen pinafores, each held up by straps and by two oval brooches. They wore woollen cloaks outside to keep out the cold. Norse women took great care of

The Viking settlement at Jarlshof in the Shetland Islands was farmed for over 400 years. Several families lived together on this site.

their hair. Archaeologists have found many of their bone combs and bronze, or silver, hair pins. Married women kept their hair covered under headscarves. Often, they wore fine chains and necklaces of beads, and hung combs, needle-cases or knives from them.

The Norse in Scotland lived close to the sea, where they found much of their food. As well as fish, they ate dead seals and whales washed up on the beaches. These gave the Norse meat and oil, as well as a good supply of bone. On the cliffs they caught sea birds for their flesh, eggs and feathers.

The Norse were good farmers. Scotland was warmer in medieval times than it is today, so barley and oats grew easily. They kept cattle, sheep, pigs, goats and poultry, so there was plenty of meat, eggs and dairy foods. They used herbs and berries in their cooking, and as medicines. The Norse drank milk when it was available. Mostly they drank weak beer made from barley. They also liked wine which they brought long distances from southern Europe.

The Norse lived in small farming villages, such as Jarlshof in the Shetland Islands. The buildings were small and simple. The walls were made of stone and turf. Whalebone and timber were used to make the frames of the roofs, which were then covered in thatch, animal skins and turf. In the centre of each house was an open fire. Heather was collected and dried to use as soft bedding. Animal skins and woollen rugs were used to make houses warmer and more comfortable.

The Orkney Jarls

The most important Norse lands in Scotland were the Orkney Islands. These were rich in good farming land and seas full of fish. The Orkney Islands provided a safe harbour for ships sailing between Norway and the Norse lands to the south in Ireland and Scotland.

In the late 800s, the Orkney Islands were used as a base by sea pirates called Vikings. Vikings were outlaws who had fled from Norway to escape punishment from a new king called Harold Finehair. The Vikings stayed on the Orkney Islands during winter, and raided Scotland, Ireland and Scandinavia in summer. In AD 874, Harold Finehair led a great expedition to the north of Scotland to destroy the Vikings. After defeating them, Harold gave the Orkney Islands to the Norwegian Earl of More, a warlord called Rognvald and his brother Sigurd. They were the first Jarls of the Orkney Islands. They had to keep the Norse lands in Scotland under control.

Viking ships had strong, quilted sails for sea voyages. The sails caught the strong sea winds which allowed the ships to reach their destinations quickly.

The first Jarls struggled to keep the Orkney Islands safe from raids by Vikings. One Jarl, called Hallad, grew tired of trying to protect the farmers from raiders who could attack suddenly, destroy a village, take the people as slaves and vanish back to sea in minutes. Hallad decided to give up his earldom. But some of the Jarls became great lords. Every year, in the summer, they collected tribute from farms and settlements around their earldom. Their power soon reached across the seas, down through the Hebrides to Galloway, and as far as the Isle of Man.

Brough of Birsay was an important Norse stronghold. Some of the buildings cannot be seen today as they have slipped into the sea over the years.

The first great Jarl was Einar, who arrived in the Orkney Islands with just one longship of warriors in AD 894. He was nicknamed Turf-Einar because he ordered the islanders to cut peat turf and dry it to use as fuel. Turf Einar fought and killed the local Viking chiefs, such as Thori Tree-Beard and Kalf Skurfa. In time, Einar became almost as powerful as the kings of Scotland and Norway.

Sigurd the Fat was another powerful Jarl. He raised a great army and went to war with Ireland. In 1014, he and his men were killed at Clontarf near Dublin fighting the Irish. Sigurd's youngest son, Thorfinn, took his father's place. Thorfinn was a rich Jarl who kept a large army feasting through the winter at his palace on Brough of Birsay, in the Orkney Islands. Although he was brave and cruel, Thorfinn became a Christian and built a church for the first bishop of the Orkney Islands. In 1048, Thorfinn made a pilgrimage to the pope in Rome, and travelled across Europe as the guest of kings and the Holy Roman Emperor.

Under Thorfinn, the earldom of the Orkney Islands reached its greatest power. It stretched across eleven earldoms in Scotland, the Hebrides and a large part of Ireland.

Feasting and Sagas

The Jarls spent their summers at sea, visiting their scattered lands to collect taxes and tribute, or to raise men for wars and adventures abroad. During the winter the Jarls stayed in their halls. In the eyes of the Norse, a great Jarl was a generous host who could feed and entertain his people well. Throughout the long, northern winter nights there would be many feasts, plenty of drinking and merriment in the Jarl's hall.

Left: A knight from the Norse chess set found on Lewis in the Hebrides. This figure was carved from a walrus tusk around AD 1150.

Above: This wooden game board dates from around AD 950. The Norse enjoyed playing board games like chess and draughts on boards like this one.

The Norse enjoyed games and sports of all kinds. One popular game was to throw stones at a small target in a circle while people cheered and put money on the result. The Swedish Northmen of Gotland may have taken their favourite sport of lifting and throwing tree trunks, or cabers, to Scotland. During quieter times, the Norse liked to play chess, and other board games using skill and strategy.

This saga was written down around AD 1300. It tells of a Viking who killed wild animals and a ferocious sea monster.

Above all, the Norse liked to hear tales of long voyages, and stories of bravery and cunning. Most of the Jarls kept a skald at his court. A skald was a poet who wrote and sang songs and tales, called sagas. These sagas were special poems that told of the great moments in the life of the Jarl and his family. The best-known skalds were able to memorize long sagas by heart, and tell the most popular stories without mistakes. These sagas were written down long after Norse times by writers in Iceland, and so they survive today.

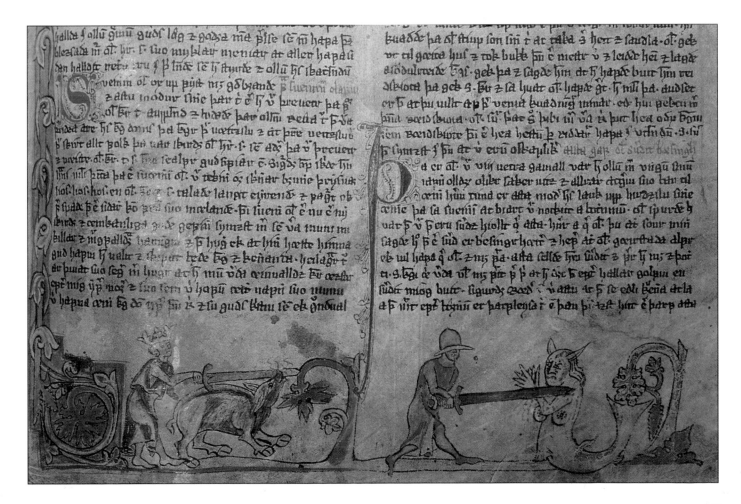

The Norse Gods of Asgard

The first Northmen to come to Scotland were Pagans. They believed in many different gods, unlike Christians who believed in only one God. The Norse gods were said to live in a heavenly place, called Asgard.

One of the gods was Wodin, who watched over the lives of men, helped by two black ravens. Warriors who died bravely in battle were taken by his ghostly shield-maidens, the Valkyries, to feast with Wodin forever in his great hall of Valhalla.

Another god, Thor, was the god who controlled the weather. To seafaring and farming folk, such as the Northmen, Thor was an important god. The Northmen believed that storms and lightning were caused by Thor angrily throwing his hammer across the skies. Norse seamen asked Thor for fair winds before setting out on long voyages. Farmers asked him to bless their soil and crops.

Frey and Freyja were gentler gods that Norse women worshipped. They watched over the homes of the Norse, and made sure that their families were healthy. But Tiu, the god of battle, and Loki, the evil god of cunning, were violent, angry gods.

The Norse also believed that the world was full of spirits that could put curses on men and ruin them. To please the gods and the spirits, the Norse made animal and human sacrifices at their holy places. We think some Scottish and Pictish slaves were killed in this way. The early Norse in Scotland tried to live like the gods who fought and feasted in Asgard. They tried to be brave in battle and at sea, and to be generous to friends and family. People were valued for their honesty, not their wealth.

This tapestry shows one-eyed Wodin, Thor with his hammer and Frey.

Left: The god of cunning, Loki, grins on this Norse age stone.

Below: Thor hammers were worn by Vikings to bring them luck in life and battle.

The Christian monks at abbeys such as Iona were terrified by these pagans with their strange and angry gods. Slowly, however, the Norse began to learn about the Christian religion. The Norse who settled in Scotland learnt new ideas from their Gaelic neighbours who were Christian. For a while, the Norse worshipped both the Christian God and the Asgard legends. Perhaps they were not sure which would bring them better luck.

By 1050, most of the Norse in Scotland had become Christian. The men of the Orkney Islands were converted to Christianity at the point of a sword. A new king of Norway threatened to kill Jarl Sigurd and his warriors unless they worshipped as Christians. Perhaps other Norse leaders became Christian because it helped them to trade with the rest of Christian Europe. By 1100, belief in the old gods had died out. Churches were built throughout the Norse lands. The greatest of these was the cathedral of Saint Magnus in Kirkwall, which was begun in 1137. Instead of raiding, Orkney Jarls led their men on pilgrimages. In 1151, Earl Rognvald rowed his longships across the Mediterranean Sea to the holy cities of Jerusalem and Rome, to visit the shrines there. The Norse of northern Scotland were still warlike people, but no more so than other Christians who lived at that time.

Viking Warriors

Every summer, the Northmen in Scotland went raiding. The Jarls set out from the Orkney Islands and sailed around their lands, calling on the Norse farmers and their sons to join in a sea journey. Many of the Norse settlers in the Hebrides and Sutherland spent the good sailing months of summer at sea on raids.

Right: This decorated Norse sword hilt from AD 900 was found in Scotland.

Below: A Norse war helmet made of iron and bronze.

Some of the Northmen made their livings as Viking warriors or soldiers. These soldiers were called carls. Every Jarl in the Orkney Islands had a bodyguard of carls who lived with him and dined at his table. Carls were also given a share of the slaves or goods taken at the end of a battle, or on a raid. Carls were full-time soldiers, so they wore some armour. This was usually a vest made of tiny iron rings linked together, called chain mail. Chain mail was expensive and difficult to make, so most Vikings did not wear it. They went into battle, protected only by an iron helmet, and a wooden and leather shield.

Viking warriors usually fought on foot and most carried a small bow. When they went into a battle, the Vikings started firing their arrows into the enemy. Then the warriors ran quickly at them, often throwing small axes. Their favourite weapon was the sword. Some of these were given special names and were finely decorated. One Orkney Jarl, Sigurd the Fat, had a special banner carried into battle. It showed a black raven. Perhaps the raven was there to remind Sigurd's warriors of Wodin's ravens who flew over battles watching for acts of courage.

When the Vikings first came to Scotland in the 800s, it seemed they were unbeatable in battle. They attacked their Scottish and Pictish enemies without warning. They captured many of the hill-forts where the local peoples tried to defend themselves. After 1100, however, the Vikings were less successful. By then the king of the Scots had an army of armoured knights on horses. The Scots also built strong, stone castles to protect their land. The Norse captured one of these, Rothesay Castle on Bute in 1230, but most of the castles held out against them.

Rothesay Castle, captured by Northmen in AD 1230.

Norse Women

Many Scandinavian women had come to Scotland with their menfolk by the 840s. Some of the women were from noble families. They were in charge of the household and servants, especially in the summer when their husbands were away. In a Norse settlement there were also slaves and local women. This certainly happened in the Hebrides where the Norse mixed with the local Gaelic people.

Norse women had some important tasks to carry out. They had to make sure there was enough food for everyone in the settlement to last the long winter months. Meat and fish had to be treated so it would be safe to eat after a long period of time. Sometimes it was salted or smoked. The Norse also liked stockfish, which was cod that had been cleaned then left to dry. Stockfish could be stored for years, then softened by soaking it

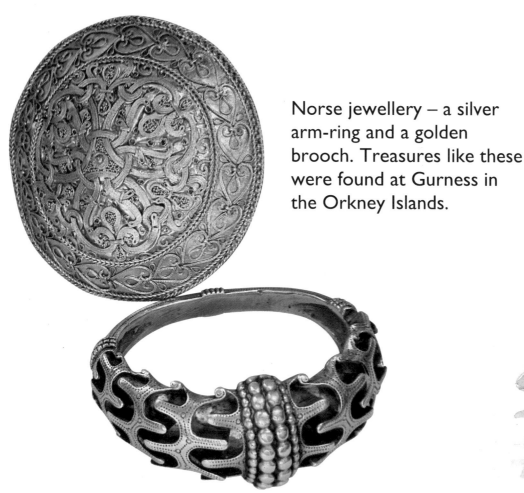

Norse jewellery – a silver arm-ring and a golden brooch. Treasures like these were found at Gurness in the Orkney Islands.

in water before cooking. Knowing how to make cloth from wool and flax was another important skill that women needed to have. Women also had to collect the heather that was used as bedding.

The grave of a Norse woman was discovered at Gurness in the Orkney Islands, in 1939. She had been laid to rest over 1,000 years ago with her jewellery and some items from her house. These items included bronze oval brooches, an iron necklet, a knife and a sickle. These were probably the objects that she liked the most.

The sagas tell us little about the life of Norse women. But one famous woman is mentioned. She was called Aud the Deep-minded. She was praised in the sagas for her cleverness. She made several dangerous journeys from Caithness to the Faroe Islands, and to Iceland where she settled with her family.

Longships and Knorrs

The Viking longships were strong, light and fast. They were ideal for raiding. The longships had strong keels so they could be dragged up on to any beach or shore. They were powered by oars, as well as a sail, so a Viking army could travel in any weather. The longships were light, and could sail up rivers or near the coast where other, heavier ships could not go.

The longships were made of long overlapping planks of timber. These were fastened together by iron rivets. The ships were waterproofed by tar or pitch. Some ships were decorated with carvings of animals or dragons.

Other Norse ships were more suited for trading. These were called knorrs. They were heavier and deeper than the warships. Knorrs were used to carry grain from the Orkney Islands to Norway. Much needed timber was taken back to the Orkney Islands on the return journey.

Norse sailors had maps and simple compasses to help them to find where they were going. At night, they used the stars to guide them. Sea captains also learnt routes from each other, memorizing important features along the coastline. The Norse preferred to sail close to land, yet made many brave voyages across the open seas.

This carving of a longship was found on a stone in Sweden.

In later years, the Norse and Gaelic people in the western islands built a new kind of Hebridean sea-galley. These galleys, or birlinns, were used for travelling around the Hebrides and for carrying troops to war on the mainland.

Below: This beautiful longship was used as a burial ship for an important Norse chief. It was discovered at Oseburg in Norway in 1904.

Above: Fierce figureheads, like this one, have been found in Viking graves. They were used to decorate Viking ships.

The End of the Norse Age

By 1100, the Norse in Scotland had changed a great deal. They had slowly lost contact with their Scandinavian cousins. They had become part of the Gaelic-speaking population. New princes, with both Norse and Gaelic blood in their veins, ruled in Scotland.

The greatest of these was called Somerled, a Norse word meaning summer wanderer. He spoke Gaelic, and led a mixed army of Norse, Irish and Scots Gaels. Somerled built a kingdom for himself in Argyll, Islay and Mull, and was the first Lord of the Isles. For some years, he was a very powerful ruler, but he died attacking Renfrew in 1164. With his death, the Norse age began to come to an end.

By 1200, the Kingdom of the Scots was winning back land from the Norsemen. The Scottish King, William the Lion, spent many summers fighting against the Norsemen on the Scottish mainland. His son, Alexander II, won back Argyll. In 1263, King Haakon of Norway sailed with a great fleet to western Scotland. After a brief fight with the Scots, Haakon's men were trapped at Largs. Many of the Northmen died from sickness and starvation. King Haakon escaped to

This is the entrance to the monument commemorating the Battle of Largs in 1263. The monument is called the pencil or needle because of its tall shape and pointed roof.

the Orkney Islands but died there soon after. In a treaty signed at Perth in 1266, his son Magnus agreed to give back control of the Hebrides to the Scots.

After 1230, the earls of the Orkney Islands were men of Scottish, not Norse, birth, but they still had to serve the kings of Norway. However, in 1468, King Christian of Norway and

The people at Largs celebrate the Scots victory every year with a festival. These men have dressed up as soldiers and are acting out the 1263 battle.

Denmark ran out of money to pay for his daughter's wedding. He sold the islands of Orkney to the Scots in 1468, and Shetland in 1469. After almost 700 years the Norse age in Scotland was over.

How do we Know About the Norse in Scotland?

The first mention of the Northmen was in books written by Christian monks at abbeys such as Iona. These monks feared the savage, pagan raiders, and only wrote about their fierceness and cruelty.

The sagas tell us much more about the Norse, their way of life and beliefs. These tales were recited aloud by skalds for centuries, around blazing winter fires in halls across the Norse kingdom. Luckily, most of the tales were written down by a great medieval poet and historian. This was Snorri Sturluson, who lived in Iceland between 1179 and 1241. Thanks to him we can read about the great men of the Norse age and learn about their bravery and cunning. Other sagas, such as the *Orkneyinga*, have only survived in part.

The Norse were only one of the many peoples that came to this country and helped to form the Scottish nation. But we still have many links today with the Viking age. Many towns have kept their Norse names. Many Highland family surnames and first names began as Norse words.

The Norse language of Norn died out in the 1700s, but some words are still used by local people in the Northern Isles. In several places in northern Scotland there are fire festivals to mark mid-winter. Young men light barrels of tar and swing, or drag, them round the town. We think this comes from the old Norse tradition of Uphalliday, a winter feast held on 29 January.

In 1874, in Lerwick in Shetland, the fire festival was banned because it was too dangerous. Instead, the young men held a torchlight procession

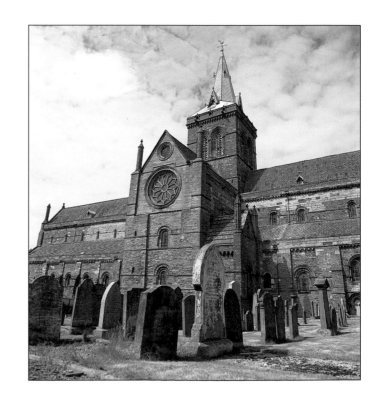

Evidence of Norse names

Scottish place name	Old Norse word
Lerwick, Wick	from 'wick' meaning bay
Dingwall	from 'thing' meaning parliament
Caithness	from 'Katanes' meaning headland of the cats
Sutherland	from 'Sudreland' meaning the land to the south
Applegarth	Norse word for apple orchard
Falkirk	from 'kirkja' meaning church

through the town. Several years later, a replica Viking longship was dragged through the town and set on fire. This became the festival of Up-Helly-Aa, held on the last Tuesday in January every year. The torchlit march of the guizers, all dressed as Vikings, is a celebration of the Shetland Islander's pride in their Norse ancestors. It is also a colourful reminder of the time when the peoples of Scandinavia ruled the northern lands and seas.

Opposite:
The cathedral of Saint Magnus in Kirkwall was one of the largest buildings in the Norse world. It was begun in 1137 by the Christian Earl Rognvald.

Right: Up-Helly-Aa. Shetlanders prepare to celebrate their Norse heritage.

Glossary

Archaeologists People who study the past by looking at objects discovered in the ground.

Borderland Land that is near the point where two or more countries meet.

Breeches Trousers worn by men, usually made of wool or leather.

Causeway A road across land which is covered by the sea when it rises.

Celtic A part of the Christian Church in Ireland and northern Britain between AD 450 and 1000.

Conquer To win property or land after a battle.

Curses Words that threaten to bring harm to a person.

Earldom The land owned and ruled by a Norse earl, or lord.

Germanic A word describing the tribal peoples of northern Europe of the Middle Ages.

Hill-fort A place of safety, usually built on a hill to make it easier to defend.

Inscriptions Norse writings, usually carved on stone.

Keels The spines or backbones of Norse ships, usually running along the entire bottom edge.

Linen Cloth made from the fibres of the flax plant. Used for clothes in Norse times.

Longships Narrow ships used by Northmen.

Pagans People who worshipped many gods.

Peat turf Layers of plants and soil that have rotted and combined together over many years. It can be dug up, dried and burned as fuel.

Picts The native peoples of northern and eastern Scotland who lived there between AD 200 and 800.

Pilgrimages Journeys to special holy places.

Rivets Iron bolts used to fasten wooden planks together when building the body of a ship.

Scots An Irish tribe who settled in western Scotland after AD 450 and who gave their name to Scotland.

Shrines Holy places where the bones of a saint are often buried.

Slaves People who are forced to work for other people against their will.

Spirits Good or evil beings which have no bodies.

Thatch Material, such as straw or reed, used for making roofs.

Tribute Payment made by a villager to a lord in exchange for protection.

Valhalla The Northmen's idea of heaven – a great hall where famous warriors feasted with the gods.

Timeline

AD 400–800 the period sometimes known as 'the Dark Ages'

795 Viking longships make their first raid on the abbey of Iona

798 Vikings raid the Hebrides

825 Vikings attack Iona looking for the magical relics of St Columba and murder the abbot, St Blathmac

830–840 Norse settle in the Orkney and Shetland Islands

850 Norse settle in Sutherland and Caithness in north Scotland

866 Olaf leads a fleet of warriors from the Viking base of Dublin in Ireland to attack the west coast of Scotland

870 Dumbarton Rock in Strathclyde is besieged by Vikings

874 Harald Finehair leads his great fleet from Norway to police the Vikings on the Orkney Islands

894 Einar the Turf cutter becomes Jarl of the Orkney Islands

980–1050 many Norse in Scotland become Christian

1000 Sigurd the Fat rules as great Jarl

1014 Sigurd dies in the bloody battle of Clontarf in Ireland

1048 Jarl Thorfinn, travels as a pilgrim to visit the pope in Rome

1040–1065 the earldom of the Orkney Islands reaches its most powerful

1101 King Edgar of Scotland pays the Norse not to attack his land

1137 Jarl Rognvald begins building Saint Magnus Cathedral in Kirkwall

1151 Rognvald leads his men on a pilgrimage

1155 Somerled rules a kingdom in the western islands of Scotland

1164 Somerled dies attacking the town of Renfrew

1200 Scottish and Norwegian royal families intermarry

1225–1240 Snorri Sturluson in Iceland writes down the Viking sagas

1230 a Norse army captures the important castle at Rothesay

1263 King Haakon IV of Norway sails with a fleet of 150 ships to try and recapture his lands in Scotland. His army perishes in the siege of Largs

1266 King Magnus gives the Hebrides to the king of the Scots

1468 Scandinavian rule ends in the Orkney Islands

1469 Scandinavian rule ends in the Shetland Islands

1700 the Norse language of Norn dies out in the Northern Isles

29

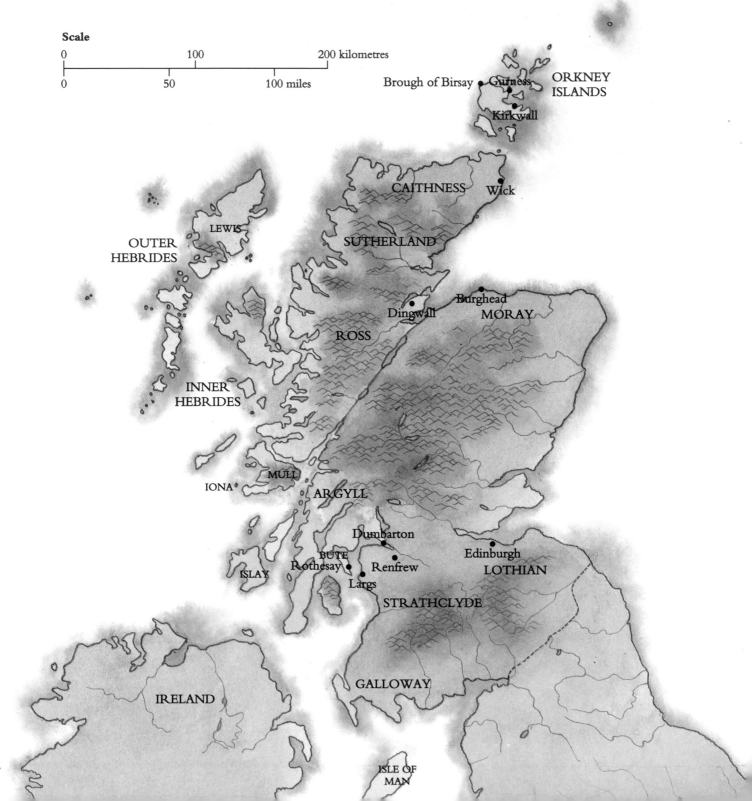

Map of Scotland

including places mentioned in the text

SHETLAND
ISLANDS

Lerwick

Jarlshof

Scale

0   100   200 kilometres

0   50   100 miles

Brough of Birsay ● ● Gurness   ORKNEY
                       ●   ISLANDS
            Kirkwall

CAITHNESS   ● Wick

LEWIS

OUTER
HEBRIDES   SUTHERLAND

                     ● Burghead
            Dingwall ●   MORAY
    ROSS

INNER
HEBRIDES

           MULL
IONA ●   ARGYLL

             Dumbarton ●
        BUTE   Edinburgh ●
  Rothesay ●   ● Renfrew   LOTHIAN
ISLAY   ● Largs
                STRATHCLYDE

             GALLOWAY

IRELAND

ISLE OF
MAN

Books to Read

For teachers:

Invaders of Scotland by Anna Ritchie and
    David Breeze (HMSO Scotland,
    1991).

Viking Scotland by Anna Ritchie
    (Batsford/Historic Scotland, 1993).

For pupils:

How would you survive as a Viking?
    by D. Salariya (Watts, 1993).

*Make This Viking Settlement: Cut-out
    Models* by I. Ashman (Usborne, 1988).

Scotland in the Middle Ages 400–1450
    by Richard Dargie (Pulse Publications,
    1995).

The Vikings: Looking into the Past
    by Jason Hook (Wayland, 1993).

Vikings: Craft Topics by Rachel Wright
    (Watts, 1992).

Viking Raiders: Time Travellers
    by A. Civardi and J. G. Campbell
    (Usborne, 1994).

Viking Warriors, Beginning History
    by Tony D. Riggs (Wayland, 1990).

Further Information

BBC Education Scotland has produced a range of resources on the Vikings.

For radio: *The Vikings*, a drama series in *Scottish Resources 7–9*.
         (Transmission Radio 3 FM, spring 1997.)
         In Gaelic: *Na Lochlannaich* in the series *Eadar Eisdeachd*.
         (Transmission Radio 3 FM, spring 1998.)

For TV: There are plans for a unit on the Vikings in Scotland in the series
         See You See Me. (Possible transmission 1997–98.)

Information on programmes and on ordering print support materials is available from:
BBC Education, Room 305, 5 Queen Street, Edinburgh EH2 1JF.
Telephone: 0131 469 4261.

Index

All numbers in **bold** refer to illustrations as well as text.